# special forces

Adam Sutherland

D1493017

First published in 2013 by Wayland

Copyright © Wayland 2013

Wayland
Hachette Children's Books
338 Euston Road
London NW1 3BH

Wayland Australia
Level 17/207 Kent Street
Sydney NSW 2000

Concept by Joyce Bentley

Commissioned by Debbie Foy and
Rasha Elsaeed

Produced for Wayland by Calcium
Designer: Paul Myerscough
Editor: Sarah Eason

British Library Cataloguing in Publication Data

Special forces. — (Police and combat)(Radar)
1. Police—Special weapons and tactics
units—Juvenile literature.
I. Series
363.2'32-dc22

ISBN: 978 0 7502 7739 6

Printed in China

Wayland is a division of Hachette Children's
Books, an Hachette UK company.

www.hachette.co.uk

Acknowledgements: Alamy: Homer Sykes
Archive 23t; Corbis: Leif Skoogfors 4–5;
Dreamstime: Vampy1 7; Flickr: Uniquely Elite
30b; iStock: Allkindza 2tc, 6; Shutterstock:
1971yes 14–15, Garret Bautista 3br, Ryan
Rodrick Beiler 11l, Ramon Berk 25bl, Sascha
Hahn back cover, Homeros 3l, 22–23,
Hurricane 2tr, 8–9, Sarah Kinnel 20–21, Kletr
25br, Leenvdb 28–29, Katarzyna Mazurowska
cover, TebNad 18–19; U.S. Army: 2b, 25bc; U.S.
Navy: 1, 2–3, 17, 26–27, 27, 31r; Wikimedia:
Folutil 10l, Saperaud 10r, U.S. Army 10r, 11r, 28,
US National Guard 12–13, US Air Force 23b.

# cover stories

# the**people**

# the**machines**

# the**moves**

# the**talk**

# THE FIGHTING ELITE

Special forces are small groups of highly skilled soldiers who are tough, intelligent and resourceful. They carry out important missions, often behind enemy lines. Here are some of the best.

## BEST OF BRITISH

The British Special Air Service (SAS) is one of the world's finest elite forces. There are about 250 SAS recruits. They are skilled in everything, from hostage rescue to intelligence gathering and anti-terrorist operations.

## ON THE WATER

The Special Boat Service (SBS) is the Royal Navy's equivalent of the SAS. Troops are drawn from the Royal Marines, and specialise in water-based operations. The SBS also gather intelligence, deal with hostage crises and provide security for important individuals.

## ACTION FORCE

Special Forces Operational Detachment-Delta, known as Delta Force, is the US Army unit in charge of fighting terrorism. Experts at freefall parachuting, hostage rescue, marksmanship and close quarter combat (CQC), members can move undetected behind enemy lines.

## UNDERWATER WARFARE

SEAL stands for Sea, Air and Land. The US elite unit specialises in amphibious operations. Troops are often dropped by boat or submarine along enemy coastlines and then swim ashore.

The dramatic announcement of Bin Laden's death made headlines around the world.

# THE HUNT FOR BIN LADEN

The world's most wanted man was captured and killed in 2011 by SEAL Team Six in northern Pakistan. But how did they find him and carry out their mission?

## LOCATING BIN LADEN

The USA had been searching for Osama Bin Laden since 9/11 (11 September 2001), the day his Al-Qaeda supporters crashed two aeroplanes into New York City's World Trade Centre, killing thousands of people. Several captured members of Al-Qaeda mentioned the name Ahmed al-Kuwaiti as one of Bin Laden's most trusted allies. The USA knew that if he was found, they would be closer to finding Bin Laden. Al-Kuwaiti was eventually tracked to a compound in Abbottabad, Pakistan. But even then, US officials were only 45 per cent sure that Bin Laden was hiding in Abbottabad.

## THE PLAN

US President Barack Obama had one of his toughest decisions to make. He could wait for more information to confirm Bin Laden's presence, bomb the building from the air, or launch a smaller-scale attack. In the end, he chose a helicopter attack to reduce the number

SEAL helicopters flew into Pakistan undetected to land at the Abbottabad compound.

of civilian casualties and to hopefully provide evidence that Bin Laden was inside. SEAL Team Six were chosen for the raid, and spent several weeks training for the attack in a full-size model of the Abbottabad compound.

## INTO BATTLE

On the night of 1 May 2011, two SEAL teams totalling 24 men arrived at the compound in two Black Hawk helicopters. One of the helicopters lost altitude and crashed, but the SEALs escaped uninjured.They entered the compound, and then killed al-Kuwaiti, Bin Laden's son, Khalid, and Bin Laden. They took Bin Laden's body, plus ten computer hard drives and other evidence and were back in the air within 38 minutes – an outstanding special forces operation.

# FIREARMS STATS!

Special forces travel and work in small groups, so their weapons are chosen to be light, powerful and reliable. Compare these handguns!

## SMITH & WESSON 340 PD

US-made short-barrel revolver, extremely light to handle and water-resistant

**Used by:** Navy SEALs

**Length:** 16 cm

**Weight:** 323 g (unloaded)

**Rate of fire:** 18 rpm

**Calibre:** 9 mm

**Number of rounds:** 5

## H&K P-10

Short-barrelled semi-automatic made in Germany since 1993

**Used by:** the German and Polish special forces

**Length:** 17.3 cm

**Weight:** 645 g (unloaded)

**Rate of fire:** 40 rpm

**Calibre:** 9 mm

**Number of rounds:** 15

## BERETTA M92F

Semi-automatic pistol designed and made in Italy since 1972

**Used by:** US special forces

**Length:** 22.3 cm

**Weight:** 954 g (unloaded)

**Rate of fire:** 40 rpm

**Calibre:** 9 mm

**Number of rounds:** 15

**KEY**
cm = centimetres
mm = millimetres
g = grams
rpm = rounds per minute

## SIG SAUER P-226

Semi-automatic pistol jointly developed between Switzerland and Germany

| | |
|---|---|
| **Used by:** | the SAS and Special Boat Service (SBS) |
| **Length:** | 19.6 cm |
| **Weight:** | 964 g |
| **Rate of fire:** | 30 rpm |
| **Calibre:** | 9 mm |
| **Number of rounds:** | 10–15 |

## FN FIVE-SEVEN

Semi-automatic pistol designed and made in Belgium since 2000

| | |
|---|---|
| **Used by:** | French, Belgian and Indian special forces |
| **Length:** | 20.8 cm |
| **Weight:** | 589 g (unloaded) |
| **Rate of fire:** | 40 rpm |
| **Calibre:** | 5.7 mm |
| **Number of rounds:** | 20 |

## GLOCK 17

Lightweight plastic semi-automatic, originally developed for the Austrian military

| | |
|---|---|
| **Used by:** | the SAS |
| **Length:** | 18.6 cm |
| **Weight:** | 625 g (unloaded) |
| **Rate of fire:** | 40 rpm |
| **Calibre:** | 9 mm |
| **Number of rounds:** | 17 |

# PASSPORT TO PROTECTION

Successful Spetsnaz candidates receive a badge with an eagle emblem (left) upon completion of their training. German special forces are trained to operate undetected behind enemy lines (above).

Most countries have a specially trained elite force, designed to fight for their country in foreign conflicts and protect against enemy attack at home. Here are some of the most influential forces from around the world.

## THE RUSSIAN SUPER FORCE

Fewer than two in ten candidates pass the Russian special forces (Spetsnaz) selection process. Around 15,000 troops work across different government departments but their job is the same – counter-terrorism and national security. The Spetsnaz GRU are the elite of the elite – a small, highly trained Russian Army unit that was formed after World War II (1939–1945) and has fought in Iraq and Afghanistan.

## GERMANY'S ELITE CORPS

The German Special Forces Command (Kommando Spezialkräfte) was formed in 1997 and is modelled on the British SAS and the US Delta Force. The unit of around 450 men has been decorated by NATO for its outstanding service in Bosnia and Kosovo during the conflicts that took

The IDF (below left) patrols the West Bank border to protect Israel from Palestinian attacks. The Japanese Special Forces Group (below) is currently serving in Iraq.

place there in the 1990s. The Special Forces Command currently has troops serving in Afghanistan.

# BATTLE IN THE MIDDLE EAST

The Israel Defense Forces (IDF) are nicknamed Duvdevan and Katzefit (meaning 'cherry' and 'cream' in English) because of their elite status. The IDF is an undercover (and often plain clothes) force that focuses on anti-terrorist operations on the West Bank (the border area between Israel and Palestine). It is known to be one of the world's most successful counter-terrorism units.

# ASIAN FORCES

The Japanese Special Forces Group (SFGp) is Japan's answer to Delta Force. This small group of just 300 soldiers

is drawn from the country's Narashino Airborne Brigade, and is responsible for protecting Japan against terrorist attacks.

# THE FORCE DOWN UNDER

The Special Air Service Regiment (SASR) in Australia is modelled on the British SAS. The three squadrons have fought in major world conflicts, including Vietnam, Iraq and Afghanistan. The regiment has two specific roles – reconnaissance and hostage rescue. The SASR also formed an important part of the security for the 2000 Sydney Olympic Games and the 2003 Rugby World Cup, which was also held in Sydney, Australia.

# BEAR GRYLLS

## THE STATS

**Name:** Edward Michael 'Bear' Grylls
**Born:** 7 June 1974
**Place of birth:** Donaghadee, Northern Ireland
**Job:** Adventurer, TV presenter

## TASTE FOR ADVENTURE

Christened Edward, but nicknamed 'Bear' by his older sister when he was just a week old, Grylls has always loved the thrill of adventure. He learned sailing and climbing from his father, and soon went in search of more thrills, from karate (he was a black belt as a teenager) to skydiving.

## IN THE SAS

After leaving school, Bear considered joining the Indian Army, and spent several months hiking in the Himalayas. He eventually joined the British Army instead, and passed the SAS selection tests – one of four successful candidates out of 180 entrants. Bear spent three years in the SAS before he broke three vertebrae in a parachuting accident. Doctors told him he came within a millimetre of damaging his spinal cord and being paralysed for life.

## ON TELEVISION

In 2005, Bear's first television series *Escape to the Legion*, followed him training in North Africa with the French Foreign Legion. The series' success led to him presenting 15 one-hour shows called *Man vs Wild*. These featured Bear parachuting into some of the world's most dangerous places and showing what you need to do to survive. *Man vs Wild* became the top cable show in the USA, and reached a global audience of more than 1.2 billion. Bear Grylls is a born survivor!

## ACTION MAN

Bear spent 18 months rehabilitating before recovering to become the youngest Briton to climb Mount Everest, at just 23 years old. The 1998 expedition took four months, and Bear was nearly killed when he fell into a 5,800-metre crevasse. After Everest, Bear then crossed the North Atlantic Ocean in an 11-metre inflatable dinghy in 2003 – braving icebergs and Force 8 gales in the world's deadliest stretch of water.

# THE HALO

High altitude, low opening (HALO) parachute jumps are an essential special forces skill. Providing weather conditions are calm, they are a fast and reliable way to get troops and equipment into enemy territory.

## Essential technique

- Clean jump from aircraft
- Act quickly to locate jumping partners in mid air
- Excellent navigation abilities to locate drop zone
- Landing skills to avoid impact injuries

## HOW IT'S DONE

1. The aircraft carrying the troops flies low into the target area to avoid being spotted on radar, then ascends quickly to allow troops to jump.
2. The teams jump at night, using oxygen masks to help them to breath in the thin atmosphere.
3. Small groups, usually four men, link together in the air by holding each other's arms. They 'fly' in this formation for considerable distances, navigating by using a compass.
4. At around 600 metres, the troops deploy their parachutes for landing.

## WHY DO IT?

HALO parachute jumps allow special force troops to land undetected in enemy territory. Most radar systems cannot detect parachutists. Troops can travel such long distances through the air that even if a HALO drop is detected, it is impossible to accurately plot where they will eventually land.

# WORLD'S BEST FIGHTERS

Special forces date back thousands of years. They were 'special' because they had more fighting experience, or better equipment and training than regular troops.

Roman emperors such as Justinian I (centre) relied on their bodyguards (pictured to his left) to protect them from assassination.

## ANCIENT BODYGUARDS

In around 550 BCE, a Persian elite group called the Immortals served as the king's bodyguard. The world's oldest fighting unit, it had 10,000 men and anyone who died in battle was replaced immediately. In ancient Rome from 280 BCE to 476 CE, the Praetorian Guard had the same role: protecting the emperor and defending the city.

## FIGHTING FOR FREEDOM

By the mid-nineteenth century, small groups with specific skills were being used in many different combat situations. In the American Civil War (1861–1965), the Confederates formed elite units whose job it was to go behind enemy lines and blow up railway lines and warehouses containing important supplies. In the second Anglo-Boer War (1899–1902), small groups of South African freedom fighters caused extensive damage and great disruption to far larger numbers of British troops.

# BRITISH ARMY IN AFRICA

The SAS was formed in 1941 by Colonel Sir David Stirling. It was made up of soldiers trained to operate in small teams behind enemy lines. Its first operation, a parachute jump into North Africa, was a disaster. One-third of the 65 men taking part were captured or killed. However, the missions that followed were far more successful. The SAS stopped operating after World War II, but quickly reformed in response to the Korean War in 1950 and the British Army fighting in Malaya (now Malaysia).

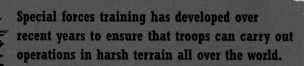

Special forces training has developed over recent years to ensure that troops can carry out operations in harsh terrain all over the world.

# WARFARE ON THE WATER

In 1962, the then US President John Kennedy commissioned the first two US Navy SEAL teams to fight in Vietnam. Their camouflage face paint meant they were known as 'the men with green faces' by the opposing Viet Cong Army. The teams specialised in gathering intelligence, and getting in and out of enemy territory without being spotted.

# The war on terror

Delta Force was formed in 1977 by Charles Beckwith, a US Army special forces officer who had spent a year training and working with the SAS. When he returned to the USA, Beckwith persuaded the US government to form a similar unit to protect against the growing threat of terrorism. Delta Force has been involved in many important operations in Iraq and the Gulf since the 1990s.

# SUPER 'COPTERS

## UH-60 BLACK HAWK

Four-bladed, twin-engine helicopter used by US, Korean and Turkish special forces

**Cruising speed:** 257 kph

**Range:** 2,200 km

**Rotor diameter:** 16.36 m

**Length:** 19.76 m

**Maximum take-off weight:** 9,900 kg

**Crew:** 4

Helicopters are the special forces' transport of choice. They are super-fast and can land on difficult terrain almost anywhere in the world!

## AH-64A APACHE

Four-blade, twin-engine attack helicopter used by UK, US, Dutch and Israeli special forces

**Cruising speed:** 284 kph

**Range:** 476 km

**Rotor diameter:** 14.63 m

**Length:** 17.73 m

**Maximum take-off weight:** 10,433 kg

**Crew:** 2

## CH-53D SEA STALLION

Transport helicopter used by German and Israeli forces and US Marines

**Cruising speed:** 278 kph

**Range:** 2,076 km

**Rotor diameter:** 24 m

**Length:** 30 m

**Maximum take-off weight:** 7,130 kg

**Crew:** 8

# AH-1W SUPER COBRA

Twin-engined attack helicopter used by US Marines, Chinese and Turkish special forces

| | |
|---|---|
| **Cruising speed:** 282 kph | |
| **Range:** 587 km | |
| **Rotor diameter:** 14.6 m | |
| **Length:** 17.7 m | |
| **Maximum take-off weight:** 6,690 kg | |
| **Crew:** 2 | |

# OH-58 KIOWA WARRIOR

Single-engine, single-rotor helicopter used by US and Israeli special forces

| | |
|---|---|
| **Cruising speed:** 204 kph | |
| **Range:** 481 km | |
| **Rotor diameter:** 10.67 m | |
| **Length:** 10.1 m | |
| **Maximum take-off weight:** 2,495 kg | |
| **Crew:** 2 | |

# SPECIAL STATS!

## 80
### PER CENT

The average dropout rate during training for special forces recruits.

## 55,000

The approximate number of special forces personnel in the USA.

## 20
### KILOGRAMS

The weight of the rucksack that special forces recruits carry for 64 kilometres as part of their selection procedure. It is equivalent to the weight of an average six-year-old child!

## 90
### METRES

The closest to the ground HALO jumpers can be before opening their parachute (less than one-third of the height of the Eiffel Tower in Paris!).

# 1,000

The number of hours a special forces recruit will spend on the firing range.

# 1:200

The ratio of Navy SEAL casualties to enemy casualties during the Vietnam War (1945–1975).

# 200,000
## KILOGRAMS

The amount of enemy explosives captured in 2001 by European special forces serving in Afghanistan.

# 30

The number of months it takes to train a Navy SEAL for his first mission.

# THE MISSIONS

Special forces operations are quick and decisive. Troops are known for taking on impossible odds and succeeding. Check out some of the most famous missions.

## 1. OPERATION NIFTY PACKAGE

In December 1989, US President Bush sent troops to invade Panama in Central America. Three Navy SEAL platoons (48 men) were given the job of capturing the country's President Manuel Noriega. Noriega's private aeroplane and gunboat were both destroyed to prevent him leaving the country, and he was eventually captured and imprisoned.

## 2. OPERATION RED DAWN

In December 2003, Task Force 121 – including members of Delta Force and the US Army Rangers – captured Iraqi President Saddam Hussein. Saddam was discovered in a one-man foxhole in the small town of ad-Dawr, armed with an AK-47 rifle and holding £450,000 (US$750,000) in cash. Saddam was tried for crimes against humanity, and given the death penalty in 2006.

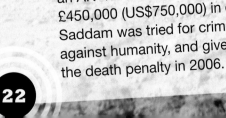

## 3. OPERATION NIMROD

In April 1980, six armed terrorists entered the Iranian Embassy in London, UK, taking 26 hostages. After five days, terrorists killed one hostage and it was decided to send in the SAS. Eight SAS men wearing gas masks and black uniforms abseiled down from the embassy roof, threw in stun grenades and tear gas canisters, and entered the building. All but one terrorist was killed, and the hostages were freed.

## 4. OPERATION BARRAS

In September 2000, 11 British soldiers were taken prisoner by rebel forces in Sierra Leone, West Africa. Five of the soldiers were soon released, but negotiations broke down and rebels threatened to kill the remaining hostages. SAS and SBS (Special Boat Service) troops were flown in to attack the rebel camps and free the British soldiers. They were in and out of the rebel camp with their mission completed in about 20 minutes!

## 5. THE BATTLE OF MOGADISHU

In October 1993, Delta Force and US Ranger teams attempted to capture the Somali warlord Mohamed Farrah Aidid. Two Black Hawk helicopters were shot down by enemy fire in the centre of rebel-held Mogadishu. The troops' amazing escape was recorded in the book *Black Hawk Down* and later made into a Hollywood film.

# DAVE THOMAS

Dave served in 21 Regiment SAS for eight years. Read on for the inside track on what being in the SAS is like, and what makes its selection procedure so tough!

## What makes an SAS man special?

You've got to have the right mental attitude. Being physically fit is very important, but operating behind enemy lines in extreme weather conditions, often with little or no sleep, and under constant threat of capture, takes mental toughness, too.

## How hard is the selection process?

Extremely hard! If you pass the first few days of gym work and interviews, you end up at a two-week selection camp. Over the first three days, you do a 22-kilometre timed walk, a 27-kilometre timed walk and then on the third day a 55-kilometre timed walk, called the 'Long Drag'. Make it through those, and you stand a chance of succeeding!

## What did you do to prepare for it?

I had read as much as I could about the SAS, so I knew it was going to be tough. I trained as best as I could – I used to go running with a 20-kilogram rucksack on my back, carrying two bricks in my hands to prepare me for the weapon I'd be carrying during real training!

## What else do you learn during training?

You have training on tactics, weapons, parachute jumps, and how to withstand enemy questioning. You are given a 'legend': a false identity that you are supposed to use when you are being interrogated. The idea is to drag out the questioning for as long as possible to increase the chance of being rescued.

**What inspires people to join the SAS?**

To be the very best. The year before I joined, 212 men took the course and only two passed! It pushes you mentally and physically to the limits – it's one of the toughest tests in the world.

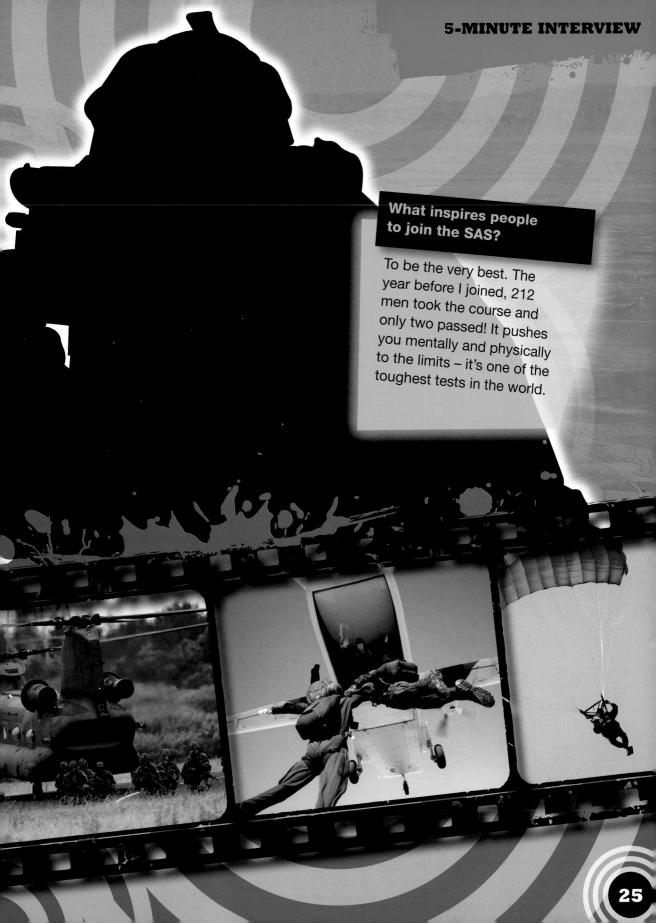

# UNDERWATER KIT

helmet

helmet

mask

Navy SEALs travel light in order to get in and out of enemy territory quickly and without being seen. Their equipment plays an important role in the success of any mission.

## HEADGEAR

When a SEAL is underwater, he wears a face mask and neoprene helmet. Out of the water, a bullet-resistant Kevlar helmet with night-vision goggles and a communications headset is standard practice. The headset allows SEALs to communicate with each other and with base camp.

flipper

## STAYING DRY

Sensitive equipment such as weapons, explosives and communication systems need to be protected in a waterproof backpack. The backpack incorporates a SEAL's breathing apparatus, and can be inflated or deflated to help divers rise to the surface or swim down to depths of up to 80 metres, depending on their mission.

rifle

## ARMED AND DANGEROUS

SEALs will usually carry a handgun – often a Smith and Wesson 340 – as well as a SEAL team knife, with a part-serrated and part-plain blade. The knife can be used in CQC, or to cut through ropes or plants that might snare a diver underwater. SEALs also often carry an M4 carbine rifle, also effective at close quarters.

The SEALs' trademark black wetsuit contains an earphone pocket in the hood so divers can communicate underwater.

27

# DELTA FORCE

Every special force has its own unique structure. This is how Delta Force is set up to successfully fight terrorism.

## THE SQUADRONS

Delta is believed to have around 1,000 members. Between 250 and 350 of them are active troops, split into three main operational squadrons. These are further broken down into troops – one troop specialising in reconnaissance and two troops trained for assault. Troops often operate in groups as small as four to six men.

# AIR PLATOONS

Supporting the three active squadrons is a helicopter platoon, which includes both attack and transport helicopters. Additional air transport is provided by the 160th Special Operations Aviation Regiment (160 SOAR). There are also back-up units dealing with training, planning and medical treatment. Delta keeps doctors at their Fort Bragg headquarters in North Carolina, as well as other secret bases around the USA, to provide medical assistance as needed.

# TROOP SUPPORT

Delta's in-house intelligence arm, Operational Support Troop (OST), is also based at Fort Bragg. It is OST's job to enter a country secretly ahead of a Delta intervention and send back information on enemy troop numbers and locations. Another important section at Fort Bragg is the Delta training facility. Details are top secret but it is believed to include shooting ranges, swimming and diving pools, and simulators for all types of counter-terrorism from trains to aeroplanes!

# COMBAT TALK

Learn some special forces lingo with our Radar guide.

**airstrike**
an attack from the air on a specific target by military aircraft

**amphibious**
military operations launched from the water against an enemy shore

**anti-terrorist/ counter-terrorism**
the methods used by governments to prevent terrorist attacks

**calibre**
the diameter of a shell or bullet

**carbine**
a lightweight rifle

**close quarter combat (CQC)**
fighting hand to hand with an enemy, often using a knife or just self-defence skills

**deploy**
to position something, usually troops or parachutes, ready for action

**foxhole**
a small pit dug to provide shelter, usually against enemy fire

**intelligence gathering**
collecting information on enemies' strengths and weaknesses, and assessing their likely future actions

**Kevlar**
a light, strong material used in army clothing

**marksmanship**
shooting skills

**mine**
an explosive device

**mortar**
a type of weapon that fires shells over short distances

**platoon**
between two and four squads of soldiers, usually led by a lieutenant (a squad contains eight to 13 soldiers)

**radar**
a system that uses radio waves to spot aircraft or other objects that are not visible to the eye

**rate of fire**
the number of rounds or bullets that can be fired from a gun each minute

**rebel forces**
an unofficial army, usually fighting for the removal of its country's government

A tough entry programme ensures only elite fighters make it into the special forces.

## reconnaissance skills

the ability to obtain information about an enemy's position

## tear gas

a non-lethal gas that temporarily irritates the eyes, nose, mouth and lungs

## stun grenades

non-lethal explosives that give off a bright flash of light and a very loud blast to temporarily affect an enemy's sight, hearing and balance

## warlord

a leader of a rebel force, who holds power through military force

# GLOSSARY

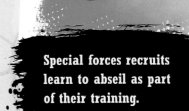

Special forces recruits learn to abseil as part of their training.

## abseil

to descend a rock face or building using ropes

## Al-Qaeda

an extreme Islamic group founded by Osama Bin Laden

## ascend

to go higher or climb

## BCE

short for before the Common Era

## CE

short for Common Era

## Confederates

the army representing the southern states of the USA during the American Civil War

## crevasse

a deep crack in rock or ice

## elite

the most powerful or skilled members of a group

## Force 8 gale

a very strong wind according to a measuring system called the Beaufort Scale

## influential

important, powerful, respected

## interrogation

being questioned with the goal of obtaining important, often secret, information

## national security

the safety of a country

## NATO

short for the North Atlantic Treaty Organisation, a group of 28 countries that work together to protect each other

## neoprene

a type of waterproof rubber, often used for wetsuits

## rehabilitating

recovering from injury or illness

## simulator

something that recreates an experience, such as a terrorist situation

## terrain

a type of ground surface

## vertebrae

the bones in the neck and back

# PREPARE FOR ACTION!

## SURF THE NET

To track down top information, arm yourself with Radar's guide!

**Navy SEALs**
Head straight to the Navy SEAL site:
**www.sealswcc.com**

**Special Operations**
Check out this fansite:
**www.specialoperations.com**

**Delta Force**
Find out more at: **http://deltaforce. americanspecialops.com**

**Dave Thomas**
Radar's expert now runs special forces training days for kids:
**www.spy-games.com/kids/kids.htm**

## READS & DOWNLOADS

Read the true story of an SAS Patrol behind enemy lines in Iraq – and one of the most famous books on the special forces ever written.
*Bravo Two Zero* by Andy McNab (Corgi, 1994)

Download a great television series called *Surviving the Cut* from iTunes and check out these other fascinating special forces apps too – *iSpecial Forces* and *Special Forces (Encyclopedia of Black Ops)*:
**www.itunes.com**

# INDEX